THE NOVELLO BOOK of

HYN

50 HYMN ARRANGEMENTS FOR
SATB CHOIR AND CONGREGATION

Edited by David Hill

Published by
Novello Publishing Limited
14-15 Berners Street,
London W1T 3LJ, UK.

Exclusive Distributors:
Music Sales Limited
Distribution Centre, Newmarket Road,
Bury St Edmunds, Suffolk IP33 3YB, UK.

Music Sales Corporation
180 Madison Avenue, 24th Floor,
New York NY 10016, USA.

Music Sales Pty Limited
Level 4, Lisgar House,
30-32 Carrington Street,
Sydney, NSW 2000 Australia.

Order No. NOV295878
ISBN 978-1-78558-311-7

Music engraved and processed by Sarah Lofthouse, SEL Music Art Ltd.
Project managed and edited by Jonathan Wikeley.

Printed in the EU.

Your Guarantee of Quality
As publishers, we strive to produce every book to the
highest commercial standards. This book has been carefully
designed to minimise awkward page turns and to make playing
from it a real pleasure. Particular care has been given to
specifying acid-free, neutral-sized paper made from pulps
which have not been elemental chlorine bleached.
This pulp is from farmed sustainable forests and was
produced with special regard for the environment.
Throughout, the printing and binding have been planned
to ensure a sturdy, attractive publication which should
give years of enjoyment. If your copy fails to meet our
high standards, please inform us and we will gladly replace it.

www.musicsalesclassical.com

THE NOVELLO BOOK *of*

HYMNS

50 HYMN ARRANGEMENTS FOR
SATB CHOIR AND CONGREGATION

Edited by David Hill

NOVELLO

CONTENTS

FOREWORD

THE ROLE OF HYMNS

The role of hymns in liturgy is central to worship within the Christian Church. From the first plainsong melodies to the most contemporary compositions, hymns are for bringing congregations, choirs and clergy into a unison voice in praise of God. There is a hymn for every occasion: this book brings together a collection of well-known hymns, to enable musicians and congregations to breathe new life and energy into their worship. Much has been done over the years to re-arrange hymns for Christmas, with David Willcocks blazing the trail in the 1960s. While there are already many publications to assist organists in playing varied harmonies, this compilation is also aimed at choirs, who can add so much to the experience of singing a hymn.

HOW TO LEAD THE CONGREGATION

The role of the organist

It is the organist's responsibility to provide confidence when introducing and accompanying a hymn. Choosing an appropriate tempo is never easy and needs much thought. Think about the speed you would wish to sing the hymn before starting to play. Be sure to maintain a steady tempo – unsteady accompaniment is disconcerting to all present and to be avoided. Practise hymns carefully beforehand – they can be challenging technically, particularly the use of pedals and the distribution of parts between the hands. Choosing a suitable registration is important, and depends on the mood and the building. Play slightly ahead of the congregation and be sure to work out the number of beats between the last chord of one verse and the first of the next before you begin. Varying the harmonies is a skill which requires practice: few are gifted with the instant ability to improvise successfully. If you wish to re-harmonise a verse, plan ahead. Though few of the organ parts in this collection are challenging, we hope you agree they will be worth spending time to ensure total confidence.

The role of the choir

Choirs should be encouraged to participate fully in the singing of hymns. It is part of their role as leaders of the worship. The arrangements in this volume are designed to inject new energy into hymn singing. Though the choral arrangements aren't difficult, choirs will need time to gain the confidence required to make an impact. It is worth working through the score with the singers to work out when they should take breaths or carry through so they can sing with greater integrity. Take time to think about the words – many of these hymns are so well-known that their meaning can become lost through their very familiarity. Think about the meaning of what you are singing, and enjoy the poetry that is set to music here.

HOW TO USE THIS COLLECTION

The hymns in this collection have been chosen to cover most of the main seasons and festivals in the church year, with the exception of Christmas. They are intended to be sung by choir and congregation, and many will work for congregation alone. To that end, although many of the arrangements look through composed, they all strictly follow the verse structure of a standard hymn, albeit in some cases with introductions and interludes between verses, and can be sung by a congregation using a hymnbook or service sheet.

Though the primary aim of this collection is to enhance and inspire the hymn-singing in a service through uplifting arrangements, in addition, these pieces can be used as simple and flexible anthems. They can all be sung in a simple version for melody plus organ, or in harmony as printed here. While there are a number of larger-scale arrangements that work as processional, first or final hymns – others are suitable for communion hymns, and we have included a number of worship songs for choirs that sing in a range of musical styles.

In almost all cases a certain amount of flexibility can be applied to the directions. All the hymns can be sung tune only; any verses for lower voices can be sung with full choir, and a number of the verses for upper voices. We hope congregations will join in these upper- and lower-voice verses – it often encourages their efforts! For those churches that print weekly service sheets, these directions can be printed in advance – for those that use hymnbooks, a simple spoken instruction before the hymn is clear. Some of the verses may be sung unaccompanied, though it is suggested that when accompanying a congregation the organist plays for every verse, to provide maximum support for the singers.

I am indebted to my colleague at Music Sales, Jonathan Wikeley, for compiling and contributing to the collection. His enthusiasm for the project has been palpable and it has been a pleasure working with him on this. To all the other contributors my thanks for providing such fine arrangements. Also thanks to Sarah Lofthouse, Martin Neary, Stephen Disley, Peter Wright, Tyrone Whiting, Rowan Kitchen and James Bowstead for their help in producing this book. We hope you enjoy the results.

David Hill
Rutland, July 2016

INDEX OF USES

for the BBC Radio 4 Ascension Day Service, St Martin-in-the-Fields, 5th May 2005

1. All hail the power of Jesu's name

CM
Edward Perronet (1726–92)

DIADEM
James Ellor (1819–99)
arr. Stephen Jackson (b. 1951)

V.1 FULL UNISON
V.2 FULL HARMONY
V.3 UPPER VOICES

1. All hail the power of Je - su's name!
2. Crown him, ye mar - tyrs of your God,
3. Ye seed of Is - rael's cho - sen race,

Let an - gels pros-trate fall, let an - gels pros - trate fall;
Who from his al - tar call, who from his al - tar call;
Ye ran - somed of the fall, ye ran - somed of the fall,

Bring forth the roy - al di - a - dem,
Ex - tol the Stem of - Jes - se's Rod,
Hail him who saves you by his grace,

And crown him,

And crown him, crown him, crown him, crown

crown him,

crown him, crown him, crown him, and crown_ him Lord of all.

him,

3.

Lord of all.

Org.

3.

𝆑 (Ped.)

𝆑

FULL VOICES 𝆑

4. Let ev - 'ry kind - red, ev - 'ry

tribe On_ this ter-rest-rial ball,_ on this_ ter - rest - rial

2. All my hope on God is founded

87 87 33 7
Robert Bridges (1844–1930)

MICHAEL
Herbert Howells (1892–1983)
arr. Meirion Wynn Jones (b. 1972)

Introduction based on Herbert Howells' *Paean* from 'Six Pieces for the Organ'

FULL VOICES

1. All my hope on God is founded; He doth still my trust re-new.

Me through change and chance he guid-eth, On-ly good and on-ly true.

God un-known, He a-lone Calls my heart to be his own.

FULL HARMONY

2. Pride of man and earth-ly glo-ry, Sword and crown be-tray his trust;

4. Dai-ly doth th'Al-migh-ty giv-er Boun-teous gifts on us be-stow;

6

What with care and toil he build-eth, Tower and tem-ple, fall to dust,
His de-sire our soul de-light-eth, Plea-sure leads us where we go.

(Straight on for V.3)
(To p.8 for V.5)

But God's power, Hour by hour, Is my tem-ple and my tower.
Love doth stand At his hand; Joy doth wait on his com-mand.

Teneramente
UPPER VOICES
mp

3. God's great good-ness aye en-dur-eth, Deep his wis-dom,

Sw. *mp*

Man.

pass - ing thought: Splen - dour, light and life at -

-tend him, Beau - ty spring - eth out of naught. Ev - er - more From his

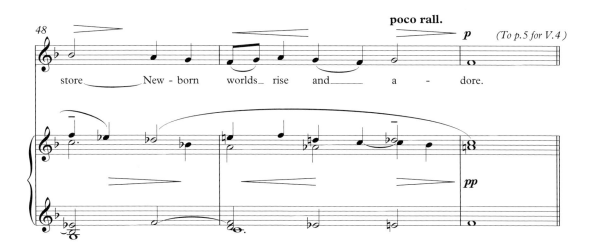

store New - born worlds rise and a - dore.

(To p.5 for V.4)

Meno mosso, con larghezza

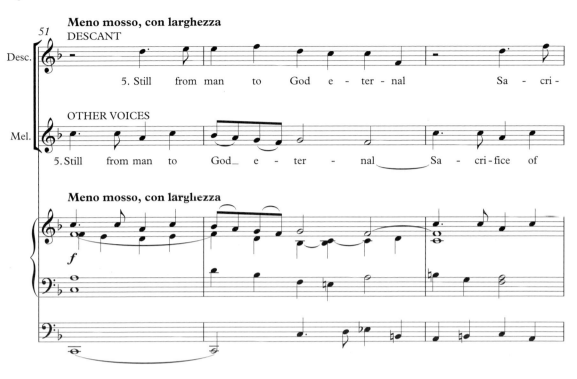

Meno mosso, con larghezza

5. Still from man to God e-ter-nal Sa-cri-

5. Still from man to God e-ter-nal Sa-cri-fice of

-fice be done, High a - bove all prais - es

praise be done, High a - bove all prais - es

prais - ing   For the gift___ of Christ___ his Son. Christ doth call___

prais - ing ___ For the gift   of Christ his Son.   Christ doth

___ all:___ Ye who fol - low___ shall___ not   fall.

call ___ One and__ all: Ye who   fol - low   shall___ not   fall.

3. All praise to thee, for thou, O King divine

10 10 10 4
Francis Bland Tucker (1895–1984)

ENGELBERG
Charles Villiers Stanford (1852–1924)
arr. David Nield (b. 1941)

1. All praise to thee, for thou, O King di-vine,____ Didst yield the

glo-ry that of right was thine,____ That in our dark-ened hearts thy

grace might shine:____ Al - le - lu - ia!

34
SOPRANO & TENOR
S.
T.
f
4. Where - fore, by God's e - ter - nal pur - pose, thou
ALTO & BASS
f
A.
B.
4. Where - fore, by God's e - ter - nal pur - pose, thou Art high ex -
f
38
Art high ex - alt - ed, And giv'n the name to which all knees shall
-alt - ed o'er all crea - tures now, And giv'n the name to which all
42
cresc.
DESCANT
f
bow: Al - le - lu - ia! Al - le - lu - ia! 5. Al - le -
OTHER VOICES
f
knees shall bow: Al - le - lu - ia! 5. Let ev - 'ry
cresc.
f

4. Alleluia, sing to Jesus

87 87 D
William Chatterton Dix (1837–98)

HYFRYDOL
Rowland Pritchard (1811–87)
arr. Richard Lloyd (b. 1933)

1. Al - le - lu - ia, sing to Je - sus! His the

scep - tre, his___ the throne; Al - le - lu - ia,

16

68
pro - mise, 'I___ am with___ you ev - er - more'?

73 **Dolcemente**
Org.
p
Man.

77
Ped.

81 ALTO
A.
mf 3. Al - le - lu - ia,
Thou on
Org.
3. Al - le - lu - ia, Bread___ of An - gels, Thou___ on
T.
B.
(melody)
mf 3. Al - le - lu - ia,
optional accompaniment

86
earth___ our food,___ our stay;___
mp
Al - le - lu - ia,
mp (melody)
Al - le - lu - ia,

91
here___ the sin - ful Flee___ to___ thee___ from day___ to___ day;

5. Amazing grace!

CM
John Newton (1725–1807)

NEW BRITAIN
Trad. American
arr. Iain Farrington (b. 1977)

6. Angel-voices ever singing

85 85 843
Francis Pott (1832–1909)

ANGEL VOICES
Edwin George Monk (1819–1900)
arr. Stephen Jackson (b. 1951)

1. An - gel - voi - ces ev - er sing - ing Round thy throne of light,

An - gel - harps for ev - er ring - ing, Rest not day nor night;

Thou-sands on - ly live to bless thee And con-fess thee Lord of might.

Back to p25 for V.4

Crafts-man's art and mu-sic's mea-sure For thy plea-sure All com - bine.

CODA

Psalm - o - dy.

DESCANT

5. Hon - our, glo - ry, me - rit Thine shall ev - er be,

OTHER VOICES

5. Hon - our, glo - ry, might and me - rit Thine shall ev - er be,

Father, Son and Spi - rit, Bless - ed Tri - ni - ty.

Father, Son and Ho - ly Spi - rit, Bless - ed Tri - ni - ty.

Of the best that thou hast giv'n, We ren - - - - der thee.

Of the best that thou hast giv - en Earth and heav - en Ren - der thee.

for the choir of St Anne's Church, Fence-in-Pendle

7. Author of life divine

66 66 88
Charles Wesley (1707–88)

RHOSYMEDRE
John Edwards (1805–85)
arr. John Bertalot (b. 1931)

This piece may also be sung with two equal voice parts.

Mellor, Lancashire
8-10th January, 2006

for Simon Vivian

8. Be still, for the presence of the Lord

15 12 12 15

Words and music:
David J. Evans (b. 1937)
arr. Stephen Jackson (b. 1951)

1. Be still, for the presence of the Lord, the Ho-ly One, is here; Come, bow be-fore him now, with re-ve-rence and fear. In him no sin is found, we stand on ho-ly ground. Be still, for the

pre-sence of the Lord, the Ho - ly One, is here.

FULL HARMONY
SOPRANO

S. 2. Be still, for the glo-ry of the Lord is shin-ing all a - round;

ALTO

A. 2. Be still, the glo - - ry shin - ing all a - round;___

TENOR

T. 2. Be still, the glo - ry is shin - ing all a - round; He

BASS

B. 2. Be still, the glo - ry is shin - ing all a - round; He___

pp optional accompaniment

Man.

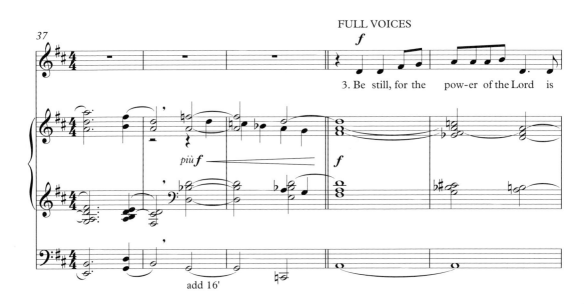

moving in this place, He comes to cleanse and heal, to minister his grace. No work too hard for him, in faith receive from him; Be still, for the power of the Lord is moving in this place.

Brockley, 24th July 2008

9a. Be thou my vision

10 11 11 11
Irish, 8th century
trans. Mary Byrne (1880–1931)
versified Eleanor Hull (1860–1935)

SLANE
Trad. Irish melody
arr. Philip Moore (b. 1943)

LOWER VOICES

2. Be thou my_ wis-dom, be_ thou my true word, Be_ thou ev - er with me, and I with thee, Lord, Be thou my_ great_ Fa - ther, and I thy true son, Be thou in me dwell - ing, and_ I with thee one.

Back to p.38 for V.5

for the Choir of All Saints, Fulham

10. Christ is made the sure foundation

87 87 87
Latin, *c.* 7th century
trans. John Mason Neale (1818–66)

WESTMINSTER ABBEY
Henry Purcell (1659–95)
arr. Jonathan Wikeley (b. 1979)

FULL HARMONY

2. All that de - di - cat - ed ci - ty, Dear - ly loved____ by
4. Here vouch - safe to__ all thy ser - vants__ Gifts of grace____ by

God__ on__ high, In ex - sul - tant__ ju - bi - la - tion__
prayer_ to__ gain; Here to have and_ hold__ for - ev - er,

Pours__ per - pe - tual me - lo - dy, God the One, in
Those__ good__ things__ their prayers_ ob - tain, And here - af - ter,

To p. 43 for V. 3
To p. 44 for V. 5

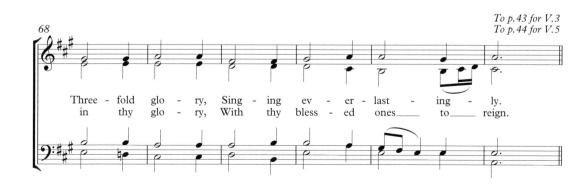

Three - fold glo - ry, Sing - ing ev - er - last - ing - ly.
in thy glo - ry, With thy bless - ed ones___ to___ reign.

44

Back to p. 42 for V. 4

be - ne - dic - tion Shed with - in its walls___ for ay.

SOPRANO 1
Al - le - lu - ia, al - le - lu - ia, al - le -

SOPRANO 2
Al - le - lu - ia, al - le - lu - ia, al - le - lu - ia, al -

ALTO
Al - le - lu - ia, al - le - lu - ia, al - le - lu - ia,

TENOR & BASS
5. Laud and ho - nour to the Fa - ther, Laud and ho - nour

(Ped.)

11. Christ triumphant, ever reigning

85 85 and refrain
Michael Saward (1932–2015)

GUITING POWER
John Barnard (b. 1948)

ORGAN

FULL VOICES

1. Christ tri - um-phant, ev - er reign-ing, Sa - viour, Mas - ter, King!
2. Word in - car - nate, truth re-veal - ing, Son of Man on earth!
3. Suf - fering ser - vant, scorned, ill-treat - ed, Vic - tim cru - ci - fied!

Lord of heaven, our lives sus-tain-ing, Hear us as we sing:
Power and ma - jes - ty con - ceal-ing By your hum - ble birth:
Death is through the cross de - feat - ed, Sin - ners just - i - fied:

Yours the glo - ry and the crown, The high re-nown, Th'e - ter - nal name.

FULL HARMONY

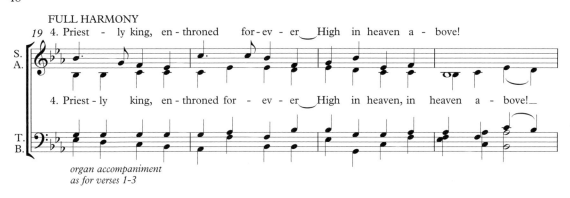

*organ accompaniment
as for verses 1-3*

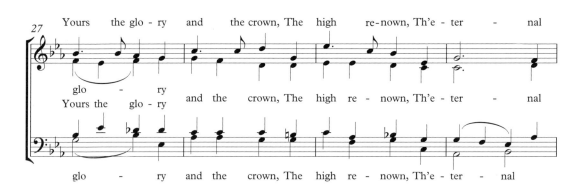

12. Come down, O Love divine

66 11 D
Italian, Bianco da Siena (*fl.* 1367–1434)
trans. Richard Frederick Littledale (1833–90)

DOWN AMPNEY
Ralph Vaughan Williams (1872–1958)
V.3 arr. Jonathan Wikeley (b. 1979)
V.4 arr. David Hill (b. 1957)

UPPER VOICES

mp

3. Let ho - ly cha - ri - ty Mine out - ward

Man.

ves - ture be, And low - li - ness be - come mine in - ner

cloth - ing; True low - li - ness of heart,

Which takes the hum - bler part, And

o'er its own short - com - ings weeps with_ loath - ing.

DESCANT

Desc.

4. And so the yearn - ing_

OTHER VOICES

Mel.

4. And so the yearn - ing strong,

Ped.

strong, With which the soul_ will long, Shall_ far out - pass the

With which the soul_ will long, Shall far out - pass the

44

pow'r of hu- man tell - ing; For_____ none can guess_ its

pow'r of hu- man tell - ing; For none can guess its

48

grace, Till he_____ be - come the place___

grace, Till he be - come the place___

52

Where - in the Ho - ly Spi - rit makes his dwell - ing.

Where - in the Ho - ly Spi - rit makes his_ dwell - ing.

13. Dear Lord and Father of mankind

86 88 6
John Whittier (1807–92)

REPTON
C. Hubert H. Parry (1848–1918)
arr. James Burton (b. 1974)

ORGAN

FULL VOICES

1. Dear Lord and Fa - ther of man- kind, For - give our fool - ish ways! Re -
2. In sim - ple trust like theirs who heard, Be - side the Sy - rian sea, The

- clothe us in our right - ful mind, In pu - rer lives thy ser - vice find, In
gra - cious call - ing of the Lord, Let us, like them, with - out a word Rise

deep - er rev - 'rence praise, in deep - er rev - 'rence praise.
up and fol - low thee, rise up and fol - low thee.

56

14. Faithful shepherd, feed me

65 65
Thomas Benson Pollock (1836–96)

PASTOR PASTORUM
Friedrich Silcher (1789–1860)
arr. William McVicker (b. 1961)

* R.H. may be played as a solo stop, if desired.

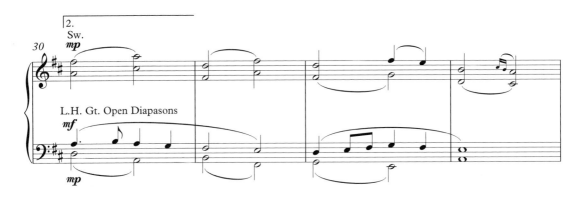

Then let an - gels bear___ me___ To thy___ pro - mised rest.

A - men, A - - men,

A - - men, A - - - men.

15. Forty days and forty nights

77 77
George Hunt Smyttan (1822–70)
and Francis Pott (1832–1909)

AUS DER TIEFE
attrib. Martin Herbst (1654–81)
arr. Harrison Oxley (1933–2009)

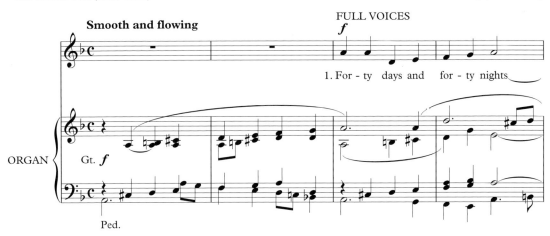

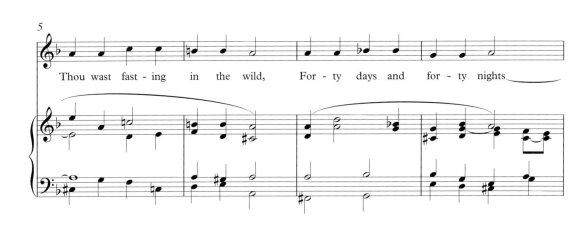

LOWER VOICES

Thou, his van-quish-er be-fore, Grant we may not faint nor fail,

5. So shall we have peace di-vine, Ho-lier glad-ness ours shall be,

Round us too shall an-gels shine, Such as mi-ni-ster'd to thee.

16. From heaven you came

The Servant King

78 78 and refrain

Words and music:
Graham Kendrick (b. 1950)
arr. Meirion Wynn Jones (b. 1972)

for Arianna

17. From the eastern mountains

65 65 D
Godfrey Thring (1823–1903)

CUDDESTON
William H. Ferguson (1874–1950)
arr. Jonathan Wikeley (b. 1979)

1. From the east-ern moun-tains Press-ing on they come, Wise men in their
2. There their Lord and Sa - viour As an in-fant lay,

wis - dom, To his hum-ble home; Stirred by deep de - vo - tion,
led them On-ward on their way, Ev - er now to light - en

Won-drous light that
Stirred by deep de - vo - tion,
Ev - er now to light - en

Hast-ing from a - far, Ev - er jour-n'ying on - ward, Guid-ed by a star.
Na-tions from a - far, As they jour - ney home-ward By that guid - ing star.

FULL HARMONY

3. Thou who in a man - ger Once had low - ly lain,
5. On - ward through the dark - ness Of the lone - ly night,

Who dost
Shin - ing

Who dost now in glo - ry O'er all king-doms reign,
Shin - ing still be - fore them With thy kind - ly light,

now in glo - ry
still be - fore them

Gath - er in the peo - ples,___ Who in lands a - far___
Guide them, Jew and Gen - tile,___ Home-ward from a - far,___

Straight on for V.4
To p.77 for V.6

Ne'er have seen the bright-ness___ Of thy guid - ing___ star.
Young and old to - geth - er, By thy guid - ing___ star.

FULL HARMONY

S.

4. Gath - er in the out - casts, All who've gone a -

A.

4. Gath - er in the out - casts,___ All who've gone a - stray,

T. *(melody)*

4. Gath - er in the out - casts, All who've gone a - stray,

B.

4. Gath - er in the out - casts, All who've gone a - stray, Throw thy

53

Back to p.74 for V.5

by the____ bright - ness___ Of thy star.

Guide them by the bright-ness___ Of thy guid - ing star.

Guide them by the bright-ness___ Of thy guid - ing star.

____ them by the bright-ness___ Of thy guid - ing____ star.

57

DESCANT

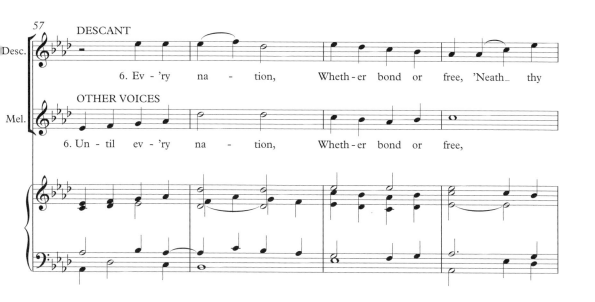

Desc.

6. Ev - 'ry na - tion, Wheth - er bond or free, 'Neath_ thy

OTHER VOICES

Mel.

6. Un - til ev - 'ry na - tion, Wheth - er bond or free,

based on the arrangement made the for the Golden Wedding Service
of the Queen and Prince Philip at Westminster Abbey on 20th November 1997

18. God save our gracious Queen

Festal setting

664 6664
Anon.

attrib. Thomas Arne (1710–78)
arr. Martin Neary (b. 1940)

80

pleased to pour, Long may she reign:

add Reeds

DESCANT
May she de - fend our laws, And ev - er___ give us cause

OTHER VOICES
May she de - fend our laws, And ev - er give us cause

To sing___ with___ heart and voice God___ save The Queen.

To sing___ with___ heart and voice God___ save The Queen.

for Tilly

19. Hark, what a sound

11 10 11 10
Frederick Myers (1843–1901)

HIGHWOOD
Richard Runciman Terry (1865–1938)
arr. Jonathan Wikeley (b. 1979)

saints_____ and to the deaf and dumb;_____ Sure - ly he com-eth, and the
I,_____ and with a hope more sweet,_____ Yearn___ for the sign, O Christ, of

earth re - joi - ces,_____ Glad in his com-ing who hath sworn, I come.
thy ful - fill - ing,_____ Faint for the flam-ing of thine ad - vent feet.

earth_ re - joi - ces, Glad_ in his_ com-ing who hath sworn,_ I come.
thy_ ful - fill - ing, Faint_ for the_ flam-ing of thine ad - vent feet.

FULL HARMONY
4. This_ hath he done,_____ and shall we not a - dore_ him? This_____ shall he

S.
A.

Org. 4. This hath he done,_____ and shall we not a - dore him? This shall he
(melody)

T.
B.

do,_ and_ can we still_ des - pair?_____ Come,_ let us quick-ly_ fling our-

Back to p.82 for V.5

- selves_ be - fore_ him,_____ Cast_ at his feet the_ bur-den of_ our care.

for Katherine

20. Hills of the North, rejoice

66 66 88
Charles E. Oakley (1832–65)
and editors of *English Praise* (1906)

LITTLE CORNARD
Martin Shaw (1875–1958)
arr. Jonathan Wikeley (b. 1979)

1. Hills of the North, re-joice, E-cho-ing songs a-rise, Hail with u-ni-ted voice
2. Isles of the South-ern seas, Sing to the list-'ning earth, Car-ry on ev-'ry breeze

Him who made earth and skies: He comes in right-eous-
Hope of a world's new birth: In Christ shall all be

21. Holy, Holy, Holy!

11 12 12 10
Reginald Heber (1783–1826)

NICAEA
John Bacchus Dykes (1823–76)
arr. Christopher Robinson (b. 1936)

33 LOWER VOICES
3. Ho - ly, Ho - ly, Ho - ly! though the dark - ness hide thee,

37
Though the eye of sin - ful man thy glo - ry may not see,

41
On - ly thou art ho - ly, there is none be - side thee

45
Per - fect in pow'r, in love, and pu - ri - ty.

for Janet

22. How Great Thou Art

11 10 11 10 and refrain
Swedish, Carl Gustav Boberg (1859–1940)
trans. Stuart K. Hine (1899–1989)

O STORE GUD
Trad. Swedish
harm. Stuart K. Hine (1899–1989)
arr. Stuart Nicholson (b. 1975)

* When singing this piece with choir only, omit bracketed sections.

94

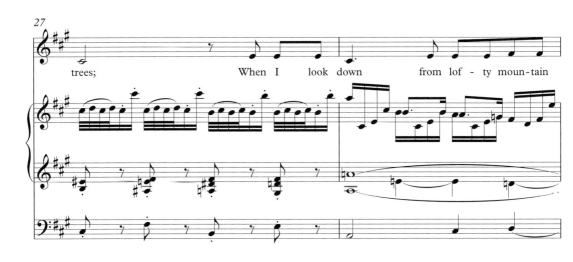

trees; When I look down from lof-ty moun-tain

gran - deur,_____ And hear the brook, and feel the gen - tle

breeze. Then sings my soul, my Sa - viour God, to

33   thee: How great thou art,   how great thou

35   art.   Then sings my soul,   my Sa - viour God, to

37   poco rit.   Meno mosso (rubato)

Thee: How great thou art,   how great thou art.

mp legato

UPPER VOICES

3. And when I

(Man.)

think that God, his Son not spar - ing,____ Sent him to die, I scarce can take it

poco rit. **poco meno mosso**

LOWER VOICES

in, That on the cross, my bur - den glad - ly

soul, my Sa - viour God, to Thee: How great thou

art, how great thou art. How great thou

FULL HARMONY

art, how great thou art.

Dublin 15th July, 2016

for the wedding of Jonna and Quinn

23. How shall I sing that majesty

DCM
John Mason (*c.* 1645–94)

COE FEN
Ken Naylor (1931–91)
harm. Jonathan Wikeley (b. 1979)
arr. Tom Wiggall (b. 1978)

1. How shall I sing that ma - jes - ty Which an - gels do_ ad - mire? Let dust in dust and si - lence lie; Sing, sing, ye heav'n - ly choir. Thou-sands of thou - sands stand a - round_Thy throne, O God most high;____ Ten thou-sand times ten thou - sand sound_Thy praise; but who_ am I?

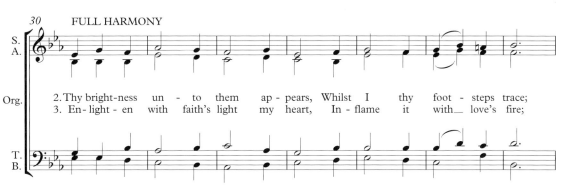

2. Thy bright-ness un - to them ap - pears, Whilst I thy foot - steps trace;
3. En - light - en with faith's light my heart, In - flame it with love's fire;

A sound of God comes to my ears, But they be - hold thy face.
Then shall I sing and bear a part With that ce - les - tial choir.

They sing be - cause thou art their Sun; Lord, send a beam on me;
I shall, I fear, be dark and cold, With all my fire and light;

For where heav'n is but once be - gun There al - le - lu - ias be.
Yet when thou dost ac - cept their gold, Lord, trea - sure up my mite.

24. I cannot tell

11 10 11 10 11 10 11 12
William Young Fullerton (1857–1932)

LONDONDERRY AIR
Trad. Irish
arr. Paul Walton (b. 1977)

1. I can-not tell why he whom an-gels wor - ship___ Should stoop to love the peo-ples of the earth, Or why as shep - herd he should seek the

FULL VOICES 25

2.I can-not tell how si-lent-ly he suf - fered,___ As with his

peace he graced this place of tears, Or how his heart up-on the cross was

bro - ken,___ The crown of pain to three and thir-ty years. But this I

know, he heals the bro-ken - heart - ed,___ And stays our sin, and calms our lurk-ing

fear, And lifts the bur - den from the hea - vy

la - den,___ For yet the Sa-viour, Sa-viour of the world, is here.

FULL VOICES

3. I can-not tell how he will win the na - tions,___ How he will

claim his earth-ly he - ri - tage, How sa - tis - fy the needs and as - pi -

Man.
optional interlude

Ped.

FULL VOICES 67

4. I can-not tell how all the lands shall wor - ship,___ When at his

(Ped.)

bid - ding ev-'ry storm is stilled, Or who can

for the Cheltenham Bach Choir, Fine Arts Brass and James Brown

25. I heard the voice of Jesus say

DCM
Horatius Bonar (1808–89)

KINGSFOLD
English folksong
adapt. Ralph Vaughan Williams (1872–1958)
arr. Stephen Jackson (b. 1951)

116

I___ found in___ him___ a___ rest - ing___ place, And___ he has made___ me___
My___ thirst was___ quenched, my___ soul___ re - vived, And___ now I live___ in___

glad.

2. I

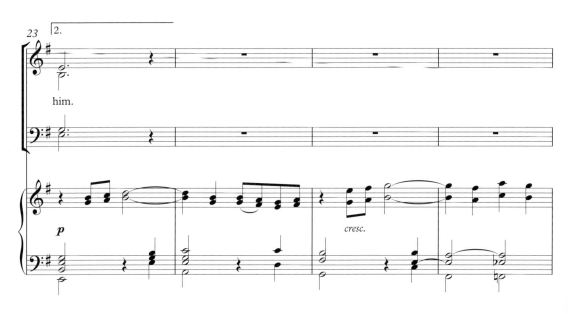

him.

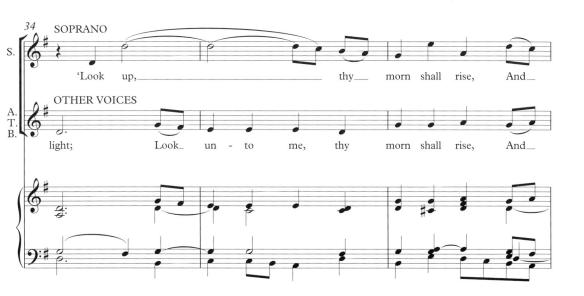

26. I, the Lord of sea and sky

77 74 D and refrain

Words and music:
Dan Schutte (b. 1947)
arr. Keith Roberts (b. 1971)

light to them? Whom shall I send? Here I am, Lord,

Is it I, Lord? I have heard you call - ing in the

night. I will go, Lord, If you lead me;

I will hold your peo - ple in my heart.

122

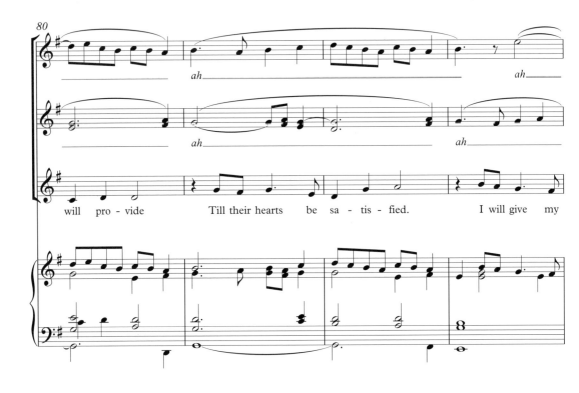

27. In Christ alone

88 88 D
Stuart Townend (b. 1963)

Keith Getty (b. 1974)
arr. Stephen Jackson (b. 1951)

128

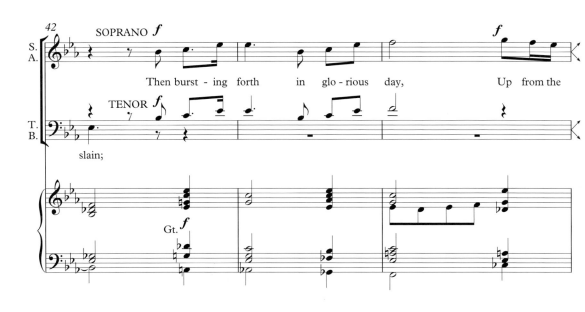

Brockley, 9th July 2016

28. It is a thing most wonderful

LM
William Walsham How (1823–97)

HERONGATE
Trad. English
harm. Ralph Vaughan Williams (1872–1958)
arr. James Burton (b. 1974)

ORGAN

FULL VOICES

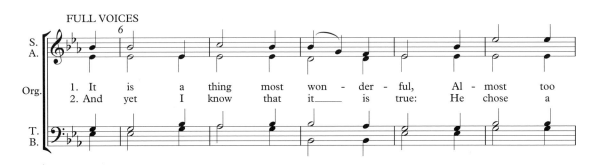

1. It is a thing most won - der - ful, Al - most too
2. And yet I know that it___ is true: He chose a

won - der - ful___ to be, That God's___ own Son___ should
poor and hum - ble lot, And wept,___ and toiled,___ and

come___ from heaven, And die to save a child___ like me.
mourned,___ and died For love of those who loved___ him not.

FULL HARMONY

3. But ev - en could__ I see__ him die, I could__ but

bear__ a lit - tle part__ Of that__ great love,__ which,

like__ a fire,__ Is al - ways burn - ing in__ his heart.

31st May 2013
Castlecroft

29. Jesus Christ is risen today

7777 and alleluias
from *Lyra Davidica* (1708)

EASTER HYMN
adapt. from a melody
in *Lyra Davidica* (1708)
arr. Matthew O'Donovan (b. 1981)

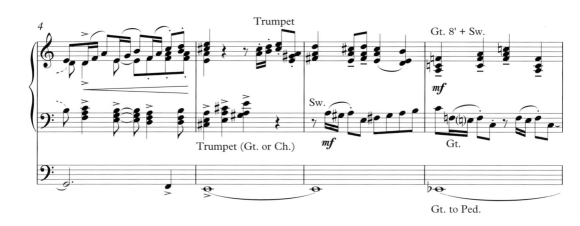

* Optional cut to bar 14. Alternatively the introduction to every verse may be omitted.

A version of this piece for organ and brass quintet is available on request from the publishers.

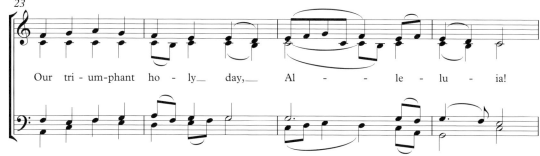

1. Je - sus Christ is ris'n to - day,__ Al - - le - lu - ia!

Our tri - um - phant ho - ly__ day,__ Al - - le - lu - ia!

Who did once, up - on the cross, Al - le - lu - ia!

Suf - fer to re - deem our loss. Al - le - lu - ia!

Org. *mf*

FULL HARMONY

Org. *f*

S.
A.

Org.

2. Hymns of praise then let us sing, Al - le - lu - ia!

T.
B.

f (Ped.)

Un - to Christ, our heav'n - ly King, Al - le - lu - ia!

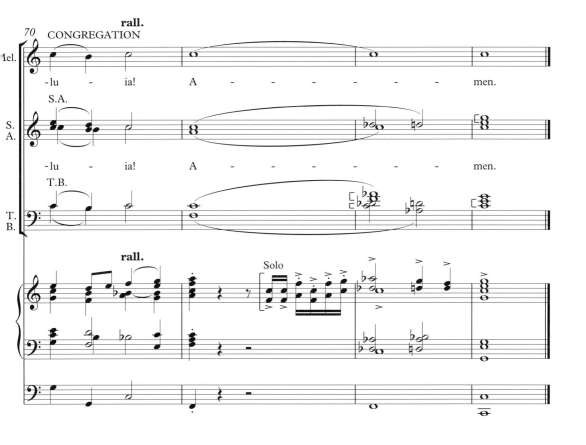

for Grace

30. Lead, kindly Light

10 4 10 4 10 10
John Henry Newman (1801–90)

ALBERTA
William Henry Harris (1883–1973)
arr. Jonathan Wikeley (b. 1979)

15

thou   me   on.   Keep thou my feet, I   do not ask to
night   is   gone,   And with the morn those an - gel fa - ces

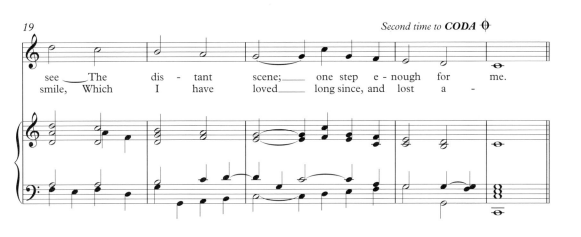

19

Second time to **CODA** ⊕

see ___ The   dis - tant   scene; ___ one step e - nough for me.
smile, Which   I   have   loved ___ long since, and lost a -

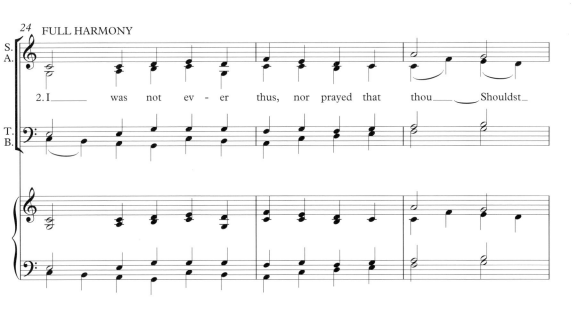

24 FULL HARMONY

S.
A.

2. I ___   was not ev - er thus, nor prayed that thou ___ Shouldst ___

T.
B.

lead_____ me on;_____ I loved to choose and

see my path, but now____ Lead____ thou____ me on._____ I

loved the gar - ish day, and, spite of fears,____ Pride____

ruled my will:____ re - mem - ber not past years.
ruled my will:____ re - mem - ber not past____ years.

ruled__ my__ will:____ re - mem - ber not past years.

⊕ CODA

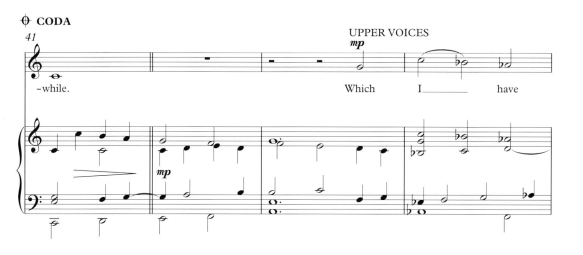

UPPER VOICES
mp

-while. Which I_____ have

mp

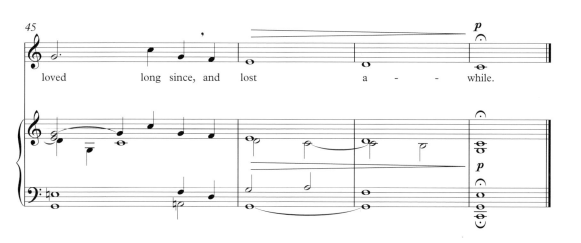

p

loved long since, and lost a - - while.

p

31. Let all mortal flesh keep silence

87 87 87
Liturgy of St James
trans. Gerard Moultrie (1829–85)

PICARDY
French carol, *c.* 17th century
from Tiersot's *Mélodies*, (Paris, 1887)
arr. Iain Farrington (b. 1977)

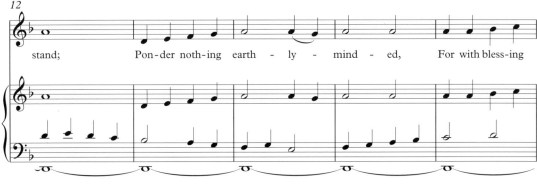

-deth, Our full ho-mage to de - mand.

2. King of kings, yet born of Ma - ry, As of old on

earth he stood, Lord of lords, in hu - man ves - ture,

In the bo-dy and the blood: He will give to all the

faith - ful___ His own self for heav'n - ly___ food.___

3. Rank on rank the host of___ heav - en___ Spreads its van - guard

on the___ way, As the Light of light des -

- cen - deth___ From the realms of end - less___ day,

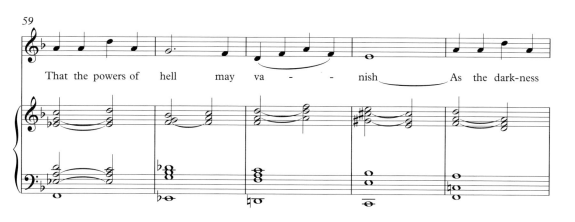

That the powers of hell may va - - nish_____ As the dark-ness

clears a - way._____

DESCANT

f

ah_____ ah_____

f OTHER VOICES

4. At his feet the six - winged_ ser - aph; Che - ru - bim with sleep - less_

ff

for the choir of York Minster, 1996

9b. Lord of all hopefulness

10 11 11 11
Jan Struther (1901–53)

SLANE
Trad. Irish melody
arr. Philip Moore (b. 1943)

LOWER VOICES

2. Lord of all__ ea - ger - ness,__ Lord of all faith, Whose__ strong hands were skilled at the plane and the lathe, Be there at__ our__ la - bours, and give us, we pray,__ Your strength in our hearts__ Lord, at the noon of the day.

York, 1996

32. Love Divine, all loves excelling

87 87 D
Charles Wesley (1707–88)

BLAENWERN
William Rowlands (1860–1937)
arr. Meirion Wynn Jones (b. 1972)

add 32' Reed

-va - tion, En - ter ev - 'ry trem - bling heart.
ceas - ing, Glo - ry in thy per - fect love.

1.

mf   *cresc.*   *f*

optional link to V.2

2.

mf

Ped.
optional link to V.3

3   3

f   Tpt. 8'   Gt.   *cresc.*
3

Tpt.   Tpt.
3   3

FULL VOICES

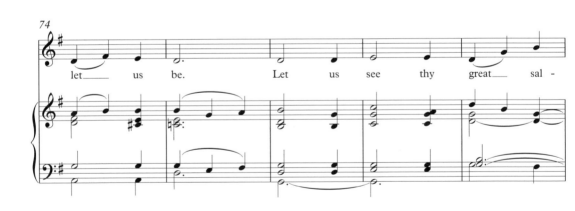

3. Fin - ish then thy new___ cre - a - tion, Pure and spot - less
let___ us be. Let us see thy great___ sal -

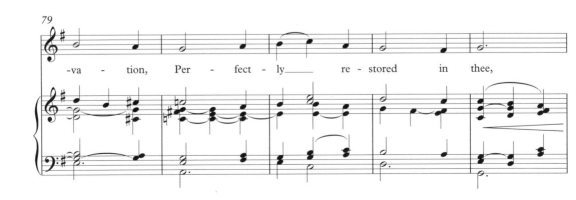

-va - tion, Per - fect - ly___ re - stored in thee,

arranged for the funeral of Diana, Princess of Wales, in Westminster Abbey, 6th September 1997

33. Make me a channel of your peace

St Francis of Assisi (1181/2–1226)
adapt. Sebastian Temple

Sebastian Temple (1928–97)
arr. Martin Neary (b. 1940)

Flowing

ORGAN

1. Make me a chan - nel of your peace: Where
2. Make me a chan - nel of your peace: Where
3. Make me a chan - nel of your peace: It

there is hat - red let me bring your love,_____ Where
there's des - pair in life let me bring hope,_____ Where
is in par - don - ing that we are par - doned, In

there is in - ju - ry, your par - don, Lord, And
there is dark - ness, on - ly_____ light, And
giv - ing of our - selves that we re - ceive, And in

34. Mine eyes have seen the glory

14 15 15 6 and refrain
Julia Ward Howe (1819–1910)

BATTLE HYMN
Trad. American
arr. Ralph Allwood (b. 1950)

ORGAN

Man.

FULL VOICES

1. Mine

eyes have seen the glo - ry of the com - ing of the Lord. He is
seen him in the watch - fires of a hun - dred cir - cling camps. They have

tramp - ling out the vin - tage where the grapes of wrath are stored. He hath
gild - ed him an al - tar in the eve - ning dews and damps. I can

loosed the fate - ful light - ning of his ter - ri - ble swift sword. His
read his right - eous sen - tence by the dim and fla - ring lamps. His

SEMICHORUS (and CONGREGATION)

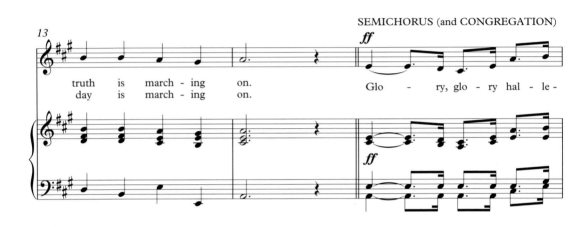

truth is march - ing on. Glo - ry, glo - ry hal - le -
day is march - ing on.

-lu - jah! Glo - ry, glo - ry hal - le - lu - jah!

Hal - le - lu - jah! Hal - le - lu - jah!

168

-lu - jah! Glo - ry, glo - ry hal - le - lu - jah!

S. & A.
Hal - le - lu - jah! Hal - le - lu - jah!

T. & B.

Glo - ry glo - ry Hal - le - lu - jah! Our God is march - ing on!

Hal - le - lu - jah! God_____ is march - ing on!

35. My song is love unknown

66 66 44 44
Samuel Crossman (1624–83)

LOVE UNKNOWN
John Ireland (1879–1962)
arr. Christopher Robinson (b. 1936)

1. My song is love un - known, My Sa-viour's love to me, Love
2. He came from his blest throne, Sal - va - tion to bes - tow: But

to the love - less shown, That they might love - ly be._____ O,
men made strange, and none The longed -for Christ_ would know._____ But

To p.173 for V.3

who am I, That for my sake_____ My Lord should take Frail flesh, and die?
O, my Friend, My Friend in-deed, Who at my need His life did spend!

4. Why, what hath my Lord done?
   What makes this rage and spite?
   He made the lame to run,
   He gave the blind their sight.
   Sweet injuries!
   Yet they at these‿
   Themselves displease,
   And 'gainst him rise.

   To p.173 for V.5

6. In life no house, no home,
   My Lord on earth might have;
   In death no friendly tomb,
   But what a stranger gave.
   What may I say?
   Heav'n was his home;
   But mine the tomb‿
   Wherein he lay.

   To p.174 for V.7

174

Back to p.172 for V.6

36. O praise ye the Lord

10 10 11 11
Henry Williams Baker (1821–77)

LAUDATE DOMINUM
C. Hubert H. Parry (1848–1918)
arr. David Hill (b. 1957)

The introduction, final verse accompaniment and Amens in this arrangement
are taken from Parry's anthem *Hear my words, ye people*.

176

Praise him who has brought you___ His___ grace from a - bove, Praise
Loud or - gans, his glo - ry___ Forth___ tell in deep___ tone, And

him who has taught___ you To sing of___ his love.
sweet harp, the sto - ry___ Of what he___ has done.

DESCANT
ff

4. Oh praise ye the Lord! Thanks - giv - ing___ and___ song____ To___

OTHER VOICES
ff

4. Oh praise ye the Lord! Thanks - giv - ing and song____ To

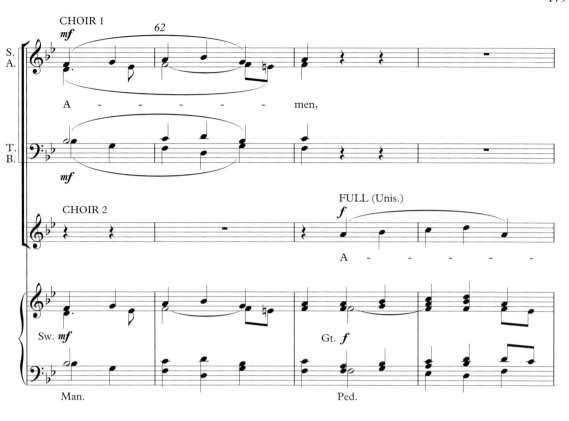

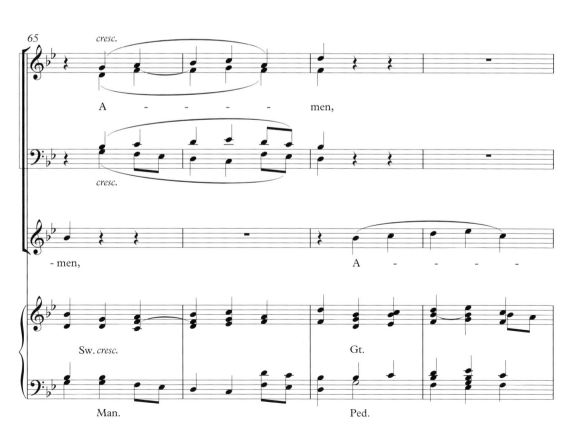

37. O thou who camest from above

LM
Charles Wesley (1707–8)

HEREFORD
Samuel Sebastian Wesley (1810–76)
arr. James Davy (b. 1980)

FULL HARMONY

3. Je - sus,___ con - firm___ my heart's___ de - sire___ To work,___ and speak,___ and think___ for thee;___ Still let me guard___ the___ ho - ly fire,___ And still___ stir up_____ thy gift_____ in me.___

DESCANT

4. Rea - dy for all thy___ per - fect___ will,___ My acts___ of

OTHER VOICES

4. Rea - dy___ for all___ thy per - fect will,___ My acts___ of

38. O worship the Lord in the beauty of holiness

13 10 13 10
John S. B. Monsell (1811–75)

WAS LEBET
Melody from *Rheinhardt MS* (1754)
arr. David Hill (b. 1957)

FULL VOICES

1. O wor-ship the Lord in the beau-ty of ho-li-ness!

Bow down be-fore him, his glo-ry pro-claim;

With gold of o-be-dience, and in-cense of low-li-ness,

Kneel and a-dore him, the Lord is his name!

ORGAN

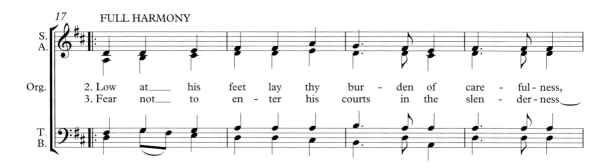

FULL HARMONY

2. Low at his feet lay thy bur - den of care - ful - ness,
3. Fear not to en - ter his courts in the slen - der - ness

High on his heart he will bear it for thee,
Of the poor wealth thou wouldst reck - on as thine:

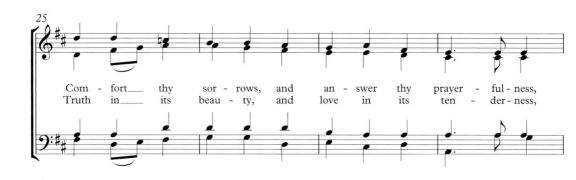

Com - fort thy sor - rows, and an - swer thy prayer - ful - ness,
Truth in its beau - ty, and love in its ten - der - ness,

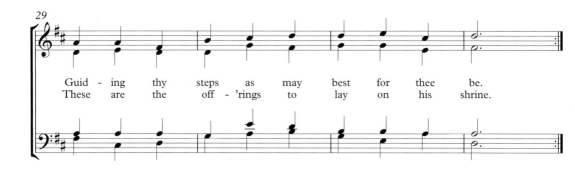

Guid - ing thy steps as may best for thee be.
These are the off - 'rings to lay on his shrine.

for my parents

39. Shine, Jesus, Shine

99 10 10 6 and refrain

Words and music:
Graham Kendrick (b. 1950)
arr. Stuart Nicholson (b. 1975)

1. Lord, the light of your love is shin - ing, In the midst of the
2. Lord, I come to your awe - some pre - sence, From the sha - dows in -

dark - ness, shin - ing; Je - sus, Light of the World, shine up - on___ us,
-to your ra - diance. By the blood I may en - ter your bright-ness,

194

Send, O send forth your word,__ O Lord, and let there be light!_____

Send forth your word,__ O Lord, and let there be light!_____

Pedal reeds (+32')

Dublin, 20th June 2016

40. Take my life, and let it be

77 77
Frances R. Havergal (1836–79)

NOTTINGHAM
Wolfgang Amadeus Mozart (1756–91)
arr. William McVicker (b. 1961)

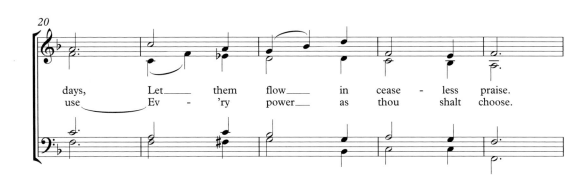

days, Let___ them flow___ in cease - less praise.
use ___ Ev - 'ry power___ as thou shalt choose.

Org.

Ped.

V.2 UPPER VOICES
V.5 LOWER VOICES

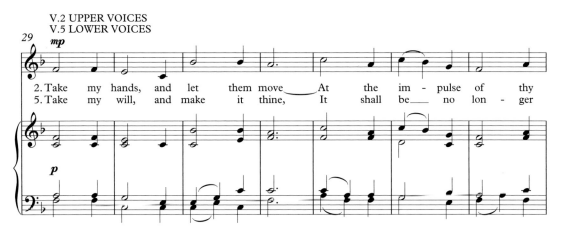

2. Take my hands, and let them move___ At the im - pulse of thy
5. Take my will, and make it thine, It shall be___ no lon - ger

love; Take my feet,__ and let them be__ Swift and beau - ti -
mine: Take my heart,__ it is thine own; It shall be__ thy

Take my self, and I will be All, all for thee.

Take my self, and I will be Ev - er, on - ly, all, for thee.

A - - - men.

41. The day thou gavest

98 98
John Ellerton (1826–93)

ST CLEMENT
Clement Scholefield (1839–1904)
arr. Christopher Robinson (b. 1936)

on - ward in - to light, Through all_ the world_ her

(Man.)

watch is keep - ing, And rests_ not now_ by day_ or night.

FULL HARMONY

S.
A.

Org. 3. As o'er_ each con - ti - nent_ and is - land The dawn_ leads

(melody)

T.
B.

(Ped.)

on_ an - oth - er day,_ The voice_ of prayer_ is

(melody)

nev - er si - lent, Nor dies___ the strain___ of praise___ a - way.

LOWER VOICES

4. The sun___ that bids___ us rest___ is wak - ing___ Our breth - ren

'neath___ the west - ern sky, And hour___ by hour___ fresh lips___ are

mak - ing___ Thy won - drous do - ings heard___ on high.

42. The first Nowell

Irregular
from William Sandys' *Christmas
Carols, Ancient and Modern* (1833)

Trad. English carol
arr. Iain Farrington (b. 1977)

43. The head that once was crowned with thorns

CM
Thomas Kelly (1769–1854)

ST MAGNUS
Jeremiah Clarke (*c.* 1673–1707)
arr. Christopher Gower (b. 1939)

5. They suf - fer with their Lord be - low, They reign with him a -

- bove, Their pro - fit and their joy to know The

mys - t'ry of his love.

44. The Lord's my shepherd

CM
Scottish Psalter (1650)

CRIMOND
Melody by Jessie Irvine (1836–87)
arr. Christopher Robinson (b. 1936)

SOPRANO
ALTO

ORGAN

TENOR
BASS

1. The Lord's my_ shep-herd,_ I'll not want; He makes_ me down_ to lie

In pas-tures green; he lead-eth_ me The qui-et wat-ers by.

UPPER VOICES

2. My soul he_ doth re-store a-gain, And me_ to walk doth make With-

Man.

-in_ the paths of right-eous-ness, E'en for_ his own name's sake.

LOWER VOICES

3. Yea, though I_ walk in_ death's dark vale; Yet will_ I fear no ill:

For thou_ art with me, and_ thy rod_ And staff_ me com - fort still.

FULL HARMONY

S.
A.

Org.

4. My ta - ble_ thou_ hast_ fur - nish - ed_ In pre - sence of_ my foes;

(melody)

T.
B.

Ped.

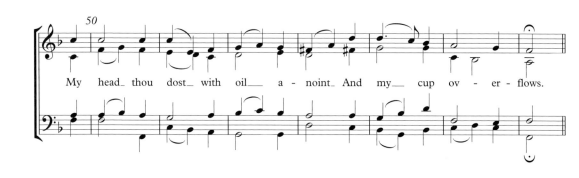

My head_ thou dost_ with oil_ a - noint_ And my_ cup ov - er - flows.

45. There is a Redeemer

Irregular

Words and music:
Melody Green (b. 1946)
arr. James Bowstead (b. 1993)

1. There is a Re - deem - er, Je - sus, God's own Son, Pre - cious Lamb of God, Mes - si - ah, Ho - ly One.

Thank you, O my Fa - ther, For giv - ing us your Son, And

32

giv-ing   us   your   Son,_____   And   leav - ing   your   Spi - rit   Till   the

36

work_ on_ earth   is   done.

p cresc.

41   DESCANT *mf*

Desc.

3. When   I   stand   in   glo - ry_____ I will see   his   face,   And

OTHER VOICES
mf

Mel.

3. When   I   stand   in   glo   -   ry____   I   will   see   his   face,_____   And

mf

46. There's a wideness in God's mercy

87 87 D
Frederick William Faber (1814–63)

CORVEDALE
Maurice Bevan (1921–2006)

1. There's a wideness in God's mercy Like the wideness of the sea; There's a kindness in his justice Which is more than liberty.

2. There is no place where earth's

sor - rows Are more felt than up in heaven; There is no place where earth's

fail - ings Have such kind-ly judge - ment given.

FULL HARMONY *p*

3. For the love of God is broad - er Than the

optional accompaniment

226

mea - sure of man's mind;__ And the heart of the E - ter - nal__ Is most

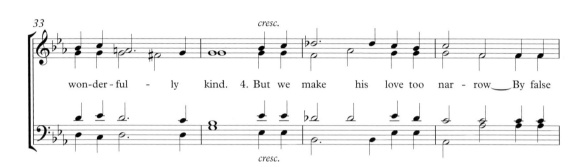

won-der-ful - ly kind. 4. But we make his love too nar - row__ By false

li - mits of our own;__ And we mag - ni - fy his strict-ness__ With a

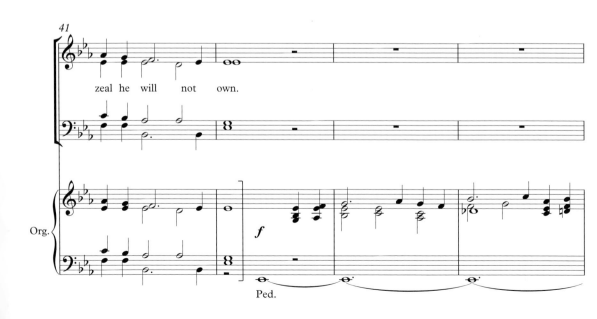

zeal he will not own.

228

47. Thine be the glory

10 11 11 11 and refrain
French, Edmund Budry (1854–1932)
trans. Richard Hoyle (1875–1939)

MACCABEUS
Georg Frideric Handel (1685–1759)
arr. Peter Miller (b. 1946)

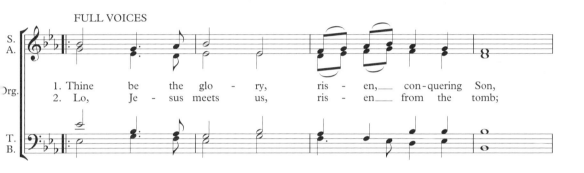

1. Thine be the glo - ry, ris - en, con-quering Son,
2. Lo, Je - sus meets us, ris - en from the tomb;

End - less is the vic - t'ry thou o'er death hast won;
Lov - ing - ly he greets us, scat - ters fear and gloom;

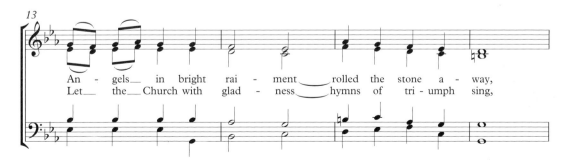

An - gels in bright rai - ment rolled the stone a - way,
Let the Church with glad - ness hymns of tri - umph sing,

Kept the folded grave-clothes where thy body lay.
For her Lord now liveth, death hath lost its sting.

Thine be the glory, risen, conquering Son,

End-less is the vic-t'ry thou o'er death hast won.

small notes organ only

won.

Tuba 8'

Sw.

Man.

Ped.

48. When I survey the wondrous cross

LM
Isaac Watts (1674–1748)

ROCKINGHAM
Edward Miller (1731–1807)
arr. Tom Wiggall (b. 1978)

To p. 234 for V. 3
To p. 235 for V. 5

UPPER VOICES

3. See from his head, his hands, his feet, Sor-

-row and love flow min - gled down!_ Did

e'er such love and sor - row meet, Or

Back to p.233 for V.4

thorns com - pose so rich_ a crown?

for Leicester Cathedral Choir, Simon Headley and the Graff Orchestra of England

49. Ye choirs of new Jerusalem

CM

Latin, St Fulbert of Chartres (d. 1028)
trans. Robert Campbell (1814–68)

ST FULBERT

Henry J. Gauntlett (1805–76)
arr. Christopher Johns (b. 1975)

50. Ye holy angels bright

66 66 44 44
Richard Baxter (1615–91)
and others

DARWALL'S 148th
John Darwall (1731–89)
arr. Keith Roberts (b. 1971)

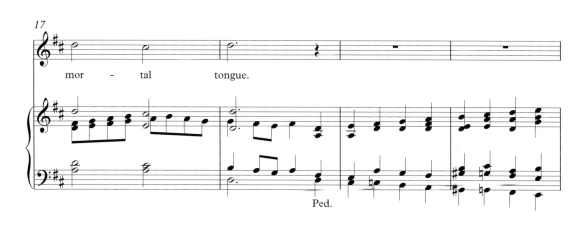

mor - tal tongue.

Ped.

FULL HARMONY

S.
A.

T.
B.

2. Ye bless-ed souls at rest, Who ran this earth-ly

race, And now, from sin re - leased, Be - hold your Sa - viour's_ face, God's

praises sound, As in his sight With sweet delight Ye do abound.

3. Ye saints, who toil below, Adore your heavenly King, And onward as ye

Now available

THE NOVELLO BOOK *of*
BRITISH
FOLKSONGS

For mixed-voice choirs

With an introduction by Jeremy Summerly

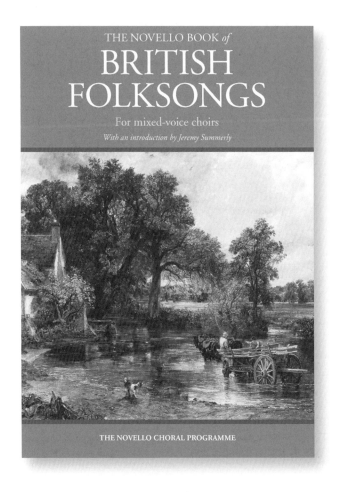

Order No. NOV164450

FRENCH SONGS & CHORUSES

for mixed-voice choir

French songs and choruses for choirs is a collection of some of the finest original choral music by French composers, and delightful arrangements of some of the greatest and most beautiful French songs. The volume is suitable for choirs of all sizes and abilities, and makes for a fine concert programme in itself, as well as being an inviting treasure trove of pieces to dip into.

Order No.: NOV165198